DANCE!
THE STATUE HAS FALLEN!
NOW HIS HEAD IS BENEATH OUR FEET!

Capener

ISBN: 978-1-913642-66-2

Cover design by Aaron Kent

Edited & Typeset by Aaron Kent

Broken Sleep Books (2021)

Broken Sleep Books Ltd
Rhydwen,
Talgarreg,
SA44 4HB
Wales

Contents

Dance! The Statue Has Fallen! Now His Head is Beneath Our Feet!   9

Coda   39
Notes   41
Acknowledgements   43

For Bristol

Dance!
The Statue Has Fallen!
Now His Head is Beneath Our Feet!

Richard Capener

The stories Bristol tells itself are written all over. On Gloucester Road, someone's graffitied INJUSTICE ANYWHERE IS A THREAT in white bubble font.

Clapping in 4/4.

Rave horns and cheers.

A thump.

Clapping in 4/4.

Rave horns and cheers.

When I was a housecleaner, my boss parked on a quiet street between jobs. I sat in the car eating my lunch as she bought hers. A woman walked while a car drove around the corner and slowed. A man in the passenger seat, no older than 30, rolled down his window and shouted, 'You fucking freak.' My boss came out of the newsagent as it happened. She got into the car and said, 'They're taking the piss out of him because he wants to be a girl.'

23:31

22:13

21:33

21:18

21:08

20:45

20:36

20:18

20:15

20:04

20:01

After redundancy from housecleaning, I temped at a warehouse in Avonmouth. The job involved unloading lorries, on arrival from manufacturers, and then loading lorries for home deliveries. There were four of us including the boss, Ginge. The team kept asking me, 'Do you know any jokes? Do you know any at all? C'mon! You must know some!' What they meant was, 'Say something racist! Our humour's predicated on reinforcing our identity! This is how we enact our hatred of the other!' A few months after I began, a twenty year old from a Chinese family joined. The team treated him like an equal. One afternoon, we were waiting at the bay for a lorry to arrive. Ginge kept asking him, 'Do you know any jokes? Do you know any?' He shook his head. Ginge began, 'What did the black man say to the Asian?'

19:59

19:54

19:45

19:44

19:43

19:39

19:36

19:30

19:28

19:28

19:24

19:23

19:22

19:20

I had a girlfriend who put us on a break because I had a one night stand with a guy years before. She demanded to be told what we had done. 'So, wait,' she said. 'You didn't give or receive anal? Oh... That's alright then.'

17:33

17:31

17:29

17:07

17:01

16:52

16:49

16:40

16:35

16:25

16:17

16:13

16:10

16:07

I saw a poster for the protest the week before. I knew I wasn't going to go. Why would I stand with homophobes and racists who think they're culturally relevant because Massive Attack were in 1991? I was selfish and jaded. I thought the city didn't care about justice. I was proud when Colston's statue toppled. The day after, I walked to Sainsbury's and saw an abandoned sign on the pavement. It read: *Silence = Violence.*

Keeping the public safe was our greatest priority and thankfully there were no instances of disorder and no arrests were made. However, there was a small group of people who clearly committed an act of criminal damage in pulling down a statue near Bristol Harbourside. An investigation will be carried out to identify those involved and we're already collating footage of the incident. I'd like to thank our partners at Bristol City Council for helping us to ensure this was a safe event for all who attended.

Politicians claimed vandalism almost immediately after Colston toppled. I remember signing petitions to have the statue removed eight years prior. Bristol Council wanted it there. Why else would it have stood so long? They refused to do the right thing then claimed the city did wrong. If this were a personal relationship, it would be called gaslighting and, like an abusive relationship, Bristol Council did it quietly. The city was never explicitly told 'vandals' were being investigated. The council needed the kudos of Bristol as the West Country's liberal capital.

15:43

15:36

15:12

15:05

15:00

14:57

14:51

14:45

14:41

14:34

14:27

14:25

The Black Lives Matter
sculpture that replaced the toppled
slaver Colston is removed

                              Bristol Council workers took
                              down the Marc Quinn sculpture of
                              BLM protester, Jen Reid, at 5.20am

Using ropes to secure the
statue before removing it and
loading it into a skip hire lorry

                              The statue was put up without
                              permission in the early hours
                              of Wednesday and lasted 24 hours

Bristol Mayor Rees tweeted:
'Anything put on the plinth outside
of the process will be removed'

                              The artwork will be held at
                              Bristol Museum for the artist to
                              collect or donate to the collection

A bloke says, 'All the way down.'

A scrape.

A bloke says, 'One… Two… Three… Go!'

Cheers.

A bloke says, 'Go on, you got it.'

Cheers.

A bloke says, 'Woah! Woah! Woah!'

Repeated clanks.

A bloke says, 'Bring it round.'

Colston should be exhibited: a historical idea to be viewed by critical gazes. But Reid? The council showed no reflection on European museums as products of colonial thinking. Reid should stand in the city centre, engaged with the rest of us. Mayor Rees stated Reid's statue was removed because it was put up 'outside of the process'. This process belongs to a system that allowed Colston to stand in the first place.

WHITE SILENCE IS VIOLENCE

BORIS IS A RACIST

I CAN'T BREATH

BLACK LIVES MATTER

SILENCE = VIOLENCE

BLACK LIVES MATTER

BLACK LIVES MATTER

SILENCE IS VIOLENCE

BLACK LIVES MATTER

HOW CAN U

BLM

BLACK LIVES MATTER

BLACK LIVES MATTER

Growing up in Gloucester, I remember when the council demolished Fred West's house. They were worried souvenir collectors would take whatever they could get. They replaced it with a smooth, grey path dotted by black bollards down the middle. Strips of grass lay either side. It looked like a thoroughfare designed by the Royal Horticultural Society.

I've written a pamphlet about Gloucester with a poem on the Fred West murders. I have as much interest in Fred and Rosemary West as I do listening to those who describe themselves as 'really into' serial killers. I don't enjoy being around them. That said, it does feel unethical to not write about the murders: it's a part of my, and the city's, experience. I took a 1995 article from The Independent and erased every word besides the names of those killed. There didn't need to be much text. Language couldn't contain all that horror.

I want to know what memorialisation is by avoiding it.

I didn't see Jen Reid's statue as memorialisation. I saw it as victory. She was what Bristol dreamt about itself for years: revolutionary, anti-authority, a champion of the people...

ENOUGH IS ENOUGH

BLACK LIVES MATTER

BLACK LIVES MATTER

BLACK LIVES MATTER

BLACK LIVES MATTER

RACISM IS A GLOBAL PANDEMIC

COLSTON MUST FALL

RACISM

BLACK LIVES MATTER

BLACK LIVES MATTER

SAY THEIR NAMES

WE

I searched the Internet for material before writing this project. News outlets like The Sun reported on the protest in a surprisingly professional way. Ginge used to read their newspaper every lunch. There were always articles on racial minorities suffering accidents that the journalist, and Ginge, found amusing, like a factory worker from Pakistan who lost his hand in a machine. The Sun's video report, however, presented stark, factual text over images of the council removing Jen Reid's statue. The chain of events (the BLM protest, Jen Reid, Bristol Council's interventions) were beginning to feel like a battle between the city itself. When Colston fell, I could hear Bristol's ancestors applaud with the crowd. I could see dead slavers retaliate through the council. A week after finding the video report, I selected the search bar on YouTube. It autosuggested, *edward colston toppled the sun.*

Is anyone going to remember Colston fell? If I name this pamphlet *Dance! The Statue has Fallen! Now His Head is Beneath Our Feet!* will readers who find it in secondhand bookstores, decades from now, think, *Ah, yes. Colston. He was a silly billy.*

In 1680 Colston became a member of the Royal African Company which at the time had a monopoly on the slave trade. By 1689 he had risen to become its deputy governor. Slaves bought in West Africa were branded with the company initials RAC, then herded on to ships and plunged into a nightmarish voyage. Closely shackled together, hundreds of enslaved people lay in their own filth; disease, suicide and murder claimed between 10 and 20 percent of them during the six to eight week voyage to the Americas. Human suffering on this scale made Colston rich and a grateful Bristol honoured his benevolence; naming dozens of buildings, institutions, charities, schools, sports clubs, pubs, societies and roads after him. His charity is commemorated during processions and church services. School children have paid homage to him at services. His statue stands in the city centre, inscribed as a 'memorial of one of the most virtuous and wise sons of the city'.

I forgot Bristol Council dredged Colston up from the harbour. They wrapped his body in what looked like blue tarpaulin, the way someone protects a car from rain.

13:39

13:36

13:30

INJUSTICE   ANYWHERE   IS   A   THREAT

I was 22 when I told my brother and sister about the sexual abuse I suffered as a child. That night, I lay under a duvet on my brother's sofa and began to have a mental breakdown. A beast with long claws swiped at my stomach, as if saying what happened conjured it.

Edward Colston's toppling is what happens when a city can't grieve. All that anger, heartbreak and trauma bursts from being held down. I'm still not sure if memorials help, with their mere marking of horror. Maybe memorialisation only happens through the body. Maybe the only way to grieve for, and with, is to stare at horror, feel upset and never stop feeling upset because no explanation will ever be good enough.

Cheers.

A bloke shouts, 'Oi! Someone say somethin'! Hang on! Hang on!'

A clank.

A splash.

Cheers.

Cheers.

Applause.

Coda

It's been eight months since I wrote the text you just read. I thought that, now, I could write a conclusion that was critically distanced, but there's almost nothing more to say about the events of June 2020. Folks have been arrested: some given cautions and fines, while four others await trial. There was a brief moment when the narrative dovetailed with the trashing of Bridewell Police Station. Rioters were demonstrating against police imposition on protests which, in part, was framed by the kidnapping and murder of a woman named Sarah Everard, for which a police officer has pleaded guilty.

It's almost too convenient, after having written a text on the failure of language to memorialise trauma, to be left with an anti-climax, not least because the plinth Colston stood on remains empty: the absence of a thing reinforcing its presence. Maybe there is a more positive place that can be gotten to. A plinth with the absence of a body might make the public aware of their own moving in relation to it and the city, which must surely be the first steps towards rewriting personal and public narratives.

When I wrote this pamphlet, I thought I was writing my break-up letter to Bristol. I'm still here, for whatever reason. Probably a mixture of convenience and financial stability. At the time of writing, in England at least, there's a little cultural calm, however fleeting. It's difficult not to feel on edge about whatever the next event will be. This bouncing back and forth between rest and unrest is testament to a public that's split in two: those who are deeply suspicious of authority, and the ignorant. I don't mean to showboat leftist politics. I sincerely don't understand how anyone can look at current authoritarian structures and think they're a good idea. It puts me in a state of needing to grieve these structures' ever-absent presence, to be aware of my body and how to act within them.

So I'm left again with silence, and the language used to talk about silence. In this moment, it's the only thing we have for each other: to be present, grieve and, in this constant state of grieving, heal. And keep grieving.

Notes

With the exception of pages 18 and 32, italicised text are audio transcriptions of mobile phone videos.

Timestamps are from Sky News' live report, *George Floyd death: Protesters and police clash for second day in central London at anti-racism demo.*

Text on page 18 was lifted from a police statement from Superintendent Andy Bennett of Avon and Somerset Police.

Text on page 21 was lifted from a video report on The Sun's YouTube channel, titled, *Bristol Council removes BLM sculpture that replaced toppled Edward Colston statue.* Two grammatical corrections were made.

Text on page 32 was lifted from Pamela Parkes' BBC article, *Who was Edward Colston and why is Bristol divided by his legacy?*

Page 24 and 29 are texts from BLM protest placards.

Acknowledgements

To Chloë Proctor, for friendship, and all the readers and contributors of *The Babel Tower Notice Board.*

To Nikki Dudley, Leia Butler, Jack Oxford, Amanda Earl and the wider literary community of which I am a part.

To Aaron Kent, and all at Broken Sleep Books, for their extraordinary work and for taking on this pamphlet.

TOPPLE YOUR UNREST